T0106699

REFLECTIONS
Through An **HOURGLASS**

A soul searching guide to finding answers to
confront your challenges in life and succeed.

E.M.Souza

InspiringVoices®
A Service of **Guideposts**

Inspiring Voices books may be ordered through booksellers or by contacting:

Inspiring Voices
1663 Liberty Drive
Bloomington, IN 47403
www.inspiringvoices.com
1-(866) 697-5313

Because of the dynamic nature of the Internet, any web addresses or links contained in this book may have changed since publication and may no longer be valid. The views expressed in this work are solely those of the author and do not necessarily reflect the views of the publisher, and the publisher hereby disclaims any responsibility for them.

Any people depicted in stock imagery provided by Thinkstock are models, and such images are being used for illustrative purposes only.

Certain stock imagery © Thinkstock.

ISBN: 978-1-4624-0067-6 (sc)
ISBN: 978-1-4624-0066-9 (e)

Library of Congress Control Number: 2012901857

Printed in the United States of America

Inspiring Voices rev. date: 3/13/2012

Contents

PART II
SLICES OF LIFE
VIGNETTES A THRU Y

PART III
ALONG LIFE'S AVENUES
POETIC VERSES

DEDICATION: This book is dedicated to men and women who in their day-to-day lives and travels around the world seek to find inspiration, and wisdom as to the substance of life. Those people who seek to make a difference in their lives and the lives of others by their selfless acts and humanitarian deeds. Those who can step up to the plate or rise to the occasion when it is deemed necessary, helping to change the tide of the times, or in your own time and way contribute to making life better in some way.

PREFACE

Author E.M.Souza takes readers on a path of rhyme and reason in Reflections through an Hourglass. You are taken on a trip down the Avenues of Life and guided to that innermost part of yourself that only you alone know. You will find yourself asking questions as to the purpose of your life, the direction it is taking, and turning over a new leaf. You will find your mirror image somewhere along that road in:

Procrastination-
How skillful you have become in allowing time to steal opportunities away from you.

Choice or Circumstance-
Makes you ponder on how you have influenced the fate or state of your life.

Old Friends-
The bonds of friendship and how important a true friend is in your life.

Hope and A Dream-
Having belief in yuour dream and the reality that it can happen.

Moving On-
Takes you out of the recurring cycle of the past and plant your feet firmly towards the future. You are steered through Loneliness and made aware of how the goal of Perseverance pays off. The loss of self-worth in being a Prisoner of someone or something. The necessity and value of Retreat on the human psyche and the art of achieving Success. It is Self-discovery!

ACKNOWLEDGMENTS

This book has awaited its birth for sometime. After many years of writing and doing personal poems and tributes for friends, co-workers and associates, its moment has arrived.

I thank my family, Antoinette, Leon and David, for their encouragement and constant moral support of me, in order that I might share this talent God has given me with the world. To my cousins, both near and far away, the rhythm of your daily lives and our memorable family reunions are all woven into the fabric of my inspiration. I treasure all the moments we have spent together.

My lifetime friends – Georgia, Tina and James whose friendship has endured over the years – you are the best!

Pauline, Dorita and Lynn who inspired me in my goals in College and Jeanie and Sister Mary who constantly reminded me that my gift of writing needed to be shared with the world.

In memory of my mother Cleonie and my father Lloyd, who set the course of my life that has brought me to do the thing I love to do the most, which is to inspire, motivate and make a difference in the lives of others. Cousin Aldin you will always be remembered for your loyalty, sincerity, kindness and love for humanity.

INTRODUCTION

The human mind, body and spirit is in constant need of an oasis to which it can constantly resort. In a world that is traveling faster than a rollercoaster, we will always find ourselves in a valley of decision.

The search for enlightenment, motivation and inspiration is the fuel that drives us and keeps us on the path we need to go. It allows us to go forward and not keep on going through the same revolving door in life.

Words that inspire us and allows us to gain insight and question ourselves, will require answers to how we look at life and what we might have to do to change our perception about many different things. Sometimes words suddenly make us surprise ourselves, in realizing somewhere along life's roll call, we have been missing a beat. We shock ourselves into admitting we were wrong or right about some things, but totally out of touch about other things, and like it or not we have to change our outlook. Such is progress, but it also tells us something about ourselves, and how essential change is in all our lives in order to move forward in the march of time.

> "When wisdom enters your heart and knowledge is pleasant to your soul, discretion will preserve you, understanding will keep you."
>
> Proverbs 2:Verse 10 & 11

> "Reflections through an Hourglass" takes you on a tour of your heart and mind to your inner being so you might look into and question, the meaning of your purpose in this life – "Every life is a Storybook".

It is a traveling companion, a bedside oasis, a gift of love(Love me now). It reflects the bonds of friendship(Old Friends) depicts the wonder of music and art(A Melody and the Dancer) Along life's avenues.

In the Vignettes we will discover that our spirit needs refreshing in (Retreat) inward introspection (Self-discovery) caught in a web of circumstances (Prisoner), all in slices of life that confront us all in many ways.

PART I

Along Life's Avenues
Poetic Verses

"Let your light shine and illuminate a path for others"

EVERY LIFE IS A STORYBOOK

Each life begins with "Once upon a Time"
And, what we make of it becomes the journal
      of our time,
The days, the moments, the years, all flashing
      past,
In a kaleidoscope of time.

How have I lived, is the question we will ask
      ourselves,
When time creeps upon us, and life becomes
      a turning wheel,
Mirroring reflections of our past.

What have I done, where have I gone?
What lessons have I learned, what lessons
      have I taught?
Have I changed someone's life, has someone's
      life changed me?

What chapter of our lives will we want to forget?
What chapter will etch itself upon our heart,
That speaks of some selfless act that makes us
      feel,
We have contributed to the measure of human
      kindness.

Yes, Every life is a storybook, and each life will
      write in it "Once upon a time".
Let your story be interesting, let it in some way
      touch the heart of mankind.
Let it in some way say – I might dance to my own
      Piper, but –
I have given life some sweet songs along the way.

A Quiet Moment

There is a quiet moment in everyone's life,
When in that moment, it is as though,
Our whole life was trapped inside a drum,
And, we start sorting out, or searching for
      answers,
Or seeking a truth serum to understand,
Why things that could have been, are not,
Or why life is not what we would expect,
And quiz ourselves as to why, or blame
      things on circumstance,
Or else turn to inventing reasons to justify
      our situation

But that quiet moment of reflection as it were,
Is like a charge of inner awareness, when we
Compare our past to our present, and wonder
      what our future might be.
It is a moment we can view our life clearly, as
      if given a second sight
And we somehow know what is wrong or what
      should be put right.
It is in that moment we realize we can no longer
      allow the winds of time
To blow our life any which way, but must take
      command,
And help along the outcome of our own destiny.

A soul searching awakening, your might say,
As if looking into a mirror and facing reality, and
Coming to terms with it, and not just letting it
      slip away.
If that quiet moment does not lend itself to changing
      the course of our life,it will make,

A contribution, by its insight, to a purpose, or at
      least be a light
Within our own darkness, to inspire us in life's
      tug-of-war,
By allowing us to use its thread of hope when the
      road here seems obscure.
In that instance when our life is thrown into a
      tailspin,
We will recall that quiet moment, surmount our
Doubts, and put our confusion and fears to rest,
All owed to that quiet moment, that time will
      envelop,
But reflection will leave imprinted in our memory.

PROCRASTINATION

Alpha and Omega,the beginning and the end.
If only life were like these two words, so simple
    and direct,
There would be no cause for decisions to arise
Nor would we have to wonder upon their effect.
But, there are times in our life, when we are caught
    somewhere in-between,
Not knowing whether to decide to go forward or back
    or stick with the same old scene.

We know whatever decision we might make, we will
    have to pay a price,
And we wonder if the decision we might make is
    worth the cost of the sacrifice.
Yet, we cannot run away from decisions, they have
    to be made sometime,
We cannot keep shoving it to the back of our heads
Or it will keep nagging at us, until something is done
    or said.

How easily we cheat ourselves, year after year,
Knowing we are stuck in the same old rut, on a road
    that is going nowhere.
We keep holding out from making decisions, trusting that
    time will solve our condition,
We say to ourselves one day we will see, to maybe
    someday it will be.
We choose to remain blind to things we know we should
    address,
Content to sit back and look at life, enslaved to conditions
    that keep us dissatisfied.

All the years we allow procrastination to stalk through
               our life,
Opportunities are passing by, and things that should be
               put right, gradually fade from sight,
Time is always tracking us and it is one we cannot measure,
And each tomorrow we face, is an empty tomorrow, if we
               just let things go astray,
Families estranged that need to be reunited, children lost
               that need to be found.
Old friends that need reaching out to, business that needs to
               be attended to.
Parents that need love and kindness, good people we meet
               everywhere who deserve appreciation.

Friends may advise us to take our life in hand, yet we overlook
               their good intentions,
By pretending we do not know what is going on, or that we just
               do not understand.
Homes that should have some harmony, in disarray, and broken
               in every way.
People stoned out of their minds, others just existing day after day.
Procrastination is never cured, by just looking the other way.
Just like the sun rises and the sun sets, it will always linger around
               until we say –
Today, I am going to do something about it, and get up and make
               that positive change.
By helping ourselves, we make others think about themselves.

FACES

Have you ever looked at faces, as if searching for a clue,
To tell you what you couldn't see, of who, or what, each
one might be?
Have you ever seen a face that scared the daylights out
of you,
And one so weather beaten, it looked like leather on a shoe?
One so wrinkled and crisscrossed, with lines all over it
like a map,
Yet another, flushed and sallow, with cheeks all sunken
in and hollow?

Haven't you seen faces all prettily dimpled, and others
with acne and pimpled,
And stunning faces that demand your gaze, while others puzzle
you like a maze?
Haven't you seen faces with odd and lost expressions, that
keep on boggling your mind?
And as you scrutinize or analyze them, you search for
answers you cannot find.
There are times you might have wondered what character lies
beyond what you perceive,
Whether it was good or bad, or could easily deceive, knowing
That there is always something more to everyone, than we
can realize.

Whether grouchy, tired and worn, caring, cynical or sadly
torn
Each face is a work of art all its own, a legacy from our birth,
a testament to our time on earth.
So let us remember how we measure others, we too are being
measured in their eyes,
And the face we each acquire was never ours to choose, just
simply bestowed on us just for a time to use

INNOCENCE

Looking at the age of innocence is seeing through the eyes
                    of a child,
Whose curiosity and learning how and why, depends on each
                    of us all the while.
Children with their trusting bonds life has not yet cut away,
Look up, to each of us to be, the footsteps here to guide their way

How could we be otherwise, than nurturing and sincere, when
We are the cornerstone of their foundation, to nurture their
                    thoughts and ideas for a future day.
How could we betray their honesty and unrelenting trust, or
Take away their innocence, and most of all, their great belief in us.

Yet, there are those who intrude upon those sacred bonds, and
Forget themselves somewhere along the line, and rob young
Children of their innocence with abuse of every kind, with,
Hurtful and demeaning words, treatment so low and mean,
Harsh and brutally exploit them and privately seduce them.

A life they would not even wish for themselves they force
Upon these innocent lives, denying them the freedom of
Childhood and the simple joys of being a child, and to learn
And discover the beauty of values and morals in a life
                    worth living.

Instead these burdened lives will live on forever trying to
                    piece together their innocence,
An interrupted childhood bearing lifelong scars, confused and,
In wonderment of how and why, with the magnitude of why
                    someone had not stepped in to save them.
Many, with someone who deeply care, have managed to put their
                    lives back together.
Time can heal bodies, but minds will always reflect, and their
                    only hope is, a purpose to go forward.
Let us then be an advocate for protecting the rights of children
By helping to guide them out of the worst of times into the best
                    of what life can offer.

Looking at Life

I know there are miracles, just as I know the sun must shine,
I know that the wind blows calm and cool, just as I know it
      can become a whirlwind too.
I know there are reasons here for you and I, just as I know
      the seasons change, I don't ask why.

I know a dawn must emerge, out of the darkest hour, just as
I know a storm must cease despite its raging power.
I know that always in the distance there is a mountain high,
Just as I know a rainbow can suddenly span the sky.

I know there are moments in every life, when turmoil seems to
      be the order of the day,
When time seems so unmoving, barely inching along its way.
But I know, like all things, these moments too, must pass,
No matter what the price we paid, or sacrifice we made,
Life gives and takes, make no mistake.

I know the poorest of lives where love is their treasure,
I know the richest of lives where sorrow and heartache lies
      in their measure,
I also know that someone down today can rise up on life's
      highest ladder,
I also know that someone, believing they captured the world,
Can see it all swirl away disappearing like a distant shadow.

I know too, that even the strong among us, have faced their
      own moments of fear and weakness,
Just as I know the weakest among us have found their
      greatest strength when needed.
I know the worst among us at times have shown themselves
      to be of some worth,
Just as I know the best among us at other times have shown
      us their very worst.

I have seen people who believed their lives hinged on the parade
  of their power,
Just fade miserably away, lost in the mist, a relic of an age past,
  a tribute to another time,
And I have seen people, who, passionate in their creed for human
  good,
The unsung heroes of our time, rise up like a shooting star,
To change the course of our history, making strides for us all.

Life is at best a miracle that will forever bewilder us all,
For although we can enjoy the tides of our fortune and fame,
We will always, whether in the heights of our glory or in the
  discourse of our discontent, remain,
Indebted to time's generosity to us, again and again.

For life asks of us, not what we amass, nor how we pursue this
  race,
But what choices we make, what lessons we learn, what message
  we gain, what love we bestow,
It is the heart and soul and spirit of us, it is that which determines
  the measure of our contribution to mankind.

WORDS

Words have a kind of power over us, to which little else
                can compare,
Except a gun, or knife, or dart, from which we might draw
                back in fear.
But, those words dispensed with grievous intent, will leave
                its mark on us, no matter what was meant.
Many a word said in haste, has triggered a scandal or disgrace
Have torn some innocent life apart, or caused some poor soul
                to lose heart.
Words have touched on some raw nerve, or invaded someone's
                secret reserve,
Or caused someone to drop dead, out of shame and worry going
                on inside their head.

Tell me then, words that cut like a knife, in time are going to fade,
And I say, you have yet to be stabbed by words, and scarred by
                the edge of its blade.
I am sure we can all remember some memorable last words, that
                lived on to become a refrain,
To haunt and echo in our brain, still alive and hammering away
With all its might, though the speaker is gone or lost to our sight,
But there are two sides to every story and sometimes words can
                just about lift you up to glory.

Think about the times you have felt down and out, and that someone
                kind, who just came around,
Think about the power of the words they said, that somehow seem
                to resurrect you from the dead,
Remember how even one word has changed the course of history,
Or how it spared the sentence of someone, imagine words of wisdom
                written by some hand,
That have endured time and still remain, instilled in our memory,
                etched in our brain.

GOLDEN OPPORTUNITY

Recognize a useful opportunity when you see it,
And seize it with both hands.
Run with it, if you have to, walk with it if you can.
Don't ever turn your back on it, without first
Weighing it over in your mind,
Search for the values in it, consider its worth in time.
Strive to find some joy in it, make it worth the effort you put into it,
Learn from it as you go along the way, gain
An ounce of wisdom from it, day by day.
Don't let your zeal outshine your principles,
In the long run it will all add up.
Take pride in your achievement, and when you look back on it,
Be able to say, it was honestly worthwhile.

A Mother's Son

Don't hand me your dreams for a race I do not want to run,
I cannot believe in them, I am not you, I am your son,
Let me discover those dreams that God has put upon my path,
I want to trace them step by step, I want to feel them in my heart.
Don't sell yourself short by saying you doubt my ability,
I am the measure of your ideals, I speak your truths, I possess
            some of your sensibility.

Let me carry my own dreams in this earthly race that I must run,
Above all let me rise to life's challenge, oppose defeat and hold
            my own triumphs in my hand.
I must learn life's lessons for that is part of life's design for
            everyone,
So, let me in my own time, and in my own way,
Give you the pleasure of saying – He truly is his mother's son.

HOPE AND A DREAM

We all have dreams of every kind, and hope sometimes
        beyond expectations.
But, as we hope, it becomes the dawn of a dream,
And when we dream, we see the vision of our hope.
And so we must not let our dream be put to flight,
Our hopes dismissed as being out of sight, as many
        hopes we least realize,
Emerges as the dream before our eyes.

How many of us have cherished a great dream,
Only to watch it dissolve unseen, knowing that hope
Had slipped away because of what someone
        had to say.
How many of us have not looked back with regret
And maybes, buts, and ifs, and yet, wondering how and
Why our dream was snatched away from us, to be
Thrown on a heap and stomped into the dust.

We look in awe at someone else's dream, knowing it was
        built on hopes, they too had seen,
Their dream kept alive, no matter what got in their way,
By hopes which made it out of the dark and into the light
        of day.
Remember the dream belongs to the dreamer, and only the
        key of Hope unlocks that door,
If you alone use that key, you must get in, hold tightly to
Hope and your dream has got to win.

FAITH

In this life we can move mountains, shake foundations,
      scale heights, conquer depths,
Light up a star, span horizons near and far, and make the
      world our oyster.
No one has been that great or been the very least, he has
Not been subject to the whole range of human emotions.
We have all wished at sometime when we were poor
      that we could be richer,
We have loved and despised, needed or wish to be needed,
Have known fear or shown courage, feel on top of the world
      or down in the dumps.
These are the cycles of our life, the phase between one link
      to the other as we explore this life.

Life is for living, along with all the risks we see, should we wish
      to turn our backs on life, day after day,
The passage of time would only swallow us whole and continue
      along its way.
It stands to reason then, that we must hold unto something strong,
      a kind of power, that will help guide us along,
What other power can be stronger than that of our faith,
It can move those mountains, shake foundations, scale heights,
Conquer depths, light up a star, span horizons near and far, and make
      the world our oyster.

WHEN LOVE IS GONE

Hanging on to someone, when you know their love for you is over,
Is above all things you can give to yourself, the unkindest cut of all.
You will have set yourself up to keep on accepting whatever is
      dished out to you,
Content in believing, and even hoping against hope, that circumstance
      will turn around for you,
While deep in your heart, you already know, that love has found
      someone else, or something new.

Yes, love can cause great happiness, but it can also inflict some pain,
When the heart once overflowing with love, finds itself empty once again.
It doesn't matter who is to blame, the fact is, the flame is burnt out, and
      it is the end of the game.
And, no amount of trying this or that. will turn it back to what it was
      once again.
When love is gone, don't try to rearrange yourself, striving in vain to please,
Doing everything within your power, even if it means going against things
      in which you believe,
Even taking leave of your senses as you desperately try to hang on, to a love
That no longer wants to hear your reasons, or do not care to understand.

Take a look at yourself and realize you are trying to turn back the clock,
Reliving old times and past memories, trying to coax old emotions back.
Admit to yourself, all the signs were there, staring you right in the face,
Perhaps in unanswered questions that teased or puzzled your mind or
In certain feelings you sensed were waning over the passing years.
Those feelings you convinced yourself, that given time would go away,
Unable to accept the fact that the person you loved, or thought you knew
      was saying goodbye to you.

We all have wishes and hopes and dreams, which are not thoughts to be
    cast aside,
They are our creative aspirations from which we are given the willpower
    to decide,
How much faith we have to challenge life, even when the odds aren't
    always on our side.
They allow us to pick up the pieces, and even give us the push we need to
    help us carry on.

Hanging on to love, when that love we know has walked away, is living
In the shadows, with our mind in yesteryear, bravely holding on to a
    lost cause in every way.
Yet amid the see-saw of our emotions, of this one thing we can be sure,
When we can see clearly through the fire and the smoke and come to terms
    with it all, in our mind,
A far stronger and wiser person can emerge, one who believes in the merits
    of self-worth.
One who knows you cannot keep hanging on because of being afraid
    of letting go, or being on your own.

As we journey through life, we have to keep an open mind, for detours or
    unexpected turns surfacing along the way,
Those flags that make us have to change our course, or cause us to ponder
    how to navigate,
To leave the road we travel, with our head still held high – When
    Love is gone.

THE UNCHANGEABLE MAN

Unchangeable Man,
Spare me your endless babble of yesterday
       and how it used to be,
You are still looking through the ledger of the
       past that you keep,
Oblivious to the present, you are still fast asleep.
You have lived every minute of every hour of
       all those years now expired.
After they did, you gave up living, you said, you
       had nothing left,
That would be worthwhile giving.

Somewhere along the road, your life lost its
       meaning,
In a mad rush, your thoughts and ideas all went
       careening,
Confused, with no longer a purpose or a goal,
Sadly, you put your life on "hold", and as you
       retreated, surrendered your soul.
Then you let yourself be bottled up, by someone
       or something that snapped the cap shut,
Content to remain in your world of yesterday,
You gave time permission to steal precious
       moments away.

How long will you keep your head buried in the
       sand,
Telling yourself new ways and changes you
       cannot understand,
Time marches on and so must we, or become
       stagnant or lost,
Forfeiting our right to be all that we should be.

Unchangeable Man,
There comes a time, when we all must bend,
There are answers to all our problems in changes
      that time will invent.
Long after you and I are gone, the moon will still
Shine and the sun still set, so each of us must make
Our life tally, in some way, in our age and time
and be counted in the steps of mankind.

OPPORTUNITIES

Opportunities are doors of chance, each door leading
       us somewhere,
And opportunities will open up to each of us, sometime,.
       someplace, somewhere.
Dropping in on us sometimes unexpectedly, taking us
       completely by surprise,
Giving us little time to consider, whether the opportunity
       would be good for us, or even wise,
Always leaving us with the burden of decision weighing
       heavily upon our minds

How do we know what appeared to be the golden opportunity,
       was really all that it seemed?
Why do we keep berating ourselves because that opportunity
       passed us by unseen?
Was it because it beckoned to us so brightly and we couldn't
       hold it within our grasp?
Or is it because it left us feeling cheated and hopelessly lost.

Why we wonder do some opportunities open up to us,
Become all that we desire, while others we pursue take us
       out of bounds,
Seemingly contrary to all that we aspire.
Still others walk us through ups and downs, twists and turns,
Before our life seems to come together,
Then suddenly things fall into place, when we least expect
And we know even if we wished, it could not have worked
       out better.

Perhaps each opportunity is a platform for lessons to be learned,
Even though we might not see it, each one is a training ground,
To add a new measure of experience that will prove useful down
       the line,
To all we may encounter, as we keep traveling on through time.

Opportunities will take us along many roads in life, some familiar
    some unknown, and,
There are opportunities that will command our attention, for
    reasons, we don't know,
But we will find out along the way, it somehow helped us grow
And with others, we will trust to our hearts to tell us when to go.

COUNTENANCE

Countenance says it all, and we should read it well.
It is clearly sending us a message, although it is
      silently conveyed,
It is a meaningful expression, a sort of silent
      confession,
A signal that, you may or may not understand,
But someone's countenance bears reasoning,
Consider it, just like you would, the cards in a
      gambler's hand.

Yet, we sometimes overlook it, or even shrug it off,
We merely acquaint it to how they might be feeling,
And fail to read the signs, that they do not welcome us,
Or there is something on their minds, something we
Might not wish to hear or know, something to make us
      feel ill at ease,
Or something that we should look into, that bears
      serious reasoning.

Quite often we could have spared ourselves from
      trouble,
And words we never wished to hear, or danger glaring
At us, while we choose to look away, if we had only
      heeded the countenance
Of some passerby or traveler, as we went upon our way.

A warm and smiling countenance can sometimes entertain
While another displays silently like neon lights, words
      that say "I want to be left alone".
All done without raising a voice, or whispering in an
      undertone,
It is the face that tells a story, and if we care to we can
      understand.
If you gaze at that face with reasoning, just as you would
      the cards in a gambler's hand.

Choice or Circumstance

When we are first put upon this earth to begin our life,
We are either born day or night, in the midst of Spring,
        Summer, Autumn or Winter.
We begin this race by status of our birth, some born
        into riches, some poor,
Some of us indulged with much, some lacking more.

We are fashioned with some beauty, or sometimes plain,
And endowed with a life force within, that's vital or
        drained.
We have the sunrise, sunset, the stars and the moon,
Lives that seemingly go on forever and lives that end all
        too soon.
We have our share of ecstasy, and our share of pain,
We lose considerably at times, or make measurable gain.

Sometimes we have to kindle   love within us, or submit
        ourselves to hate,
Is it really our choice at times, or can circumstance devise
        our fate?
Either we are striving for peace or find ourselves in conflict
        or at war,
We move to the beat of our age and time, or get lost
      in the past and left behind.
We commit to ignorance or fight to educate our minds,
We accept whatever lies before us or search for the truth
        beyond what we see.

We must make endeavors to succeed, or we will easily bow
        down to defeat,
Nurture the strength we have, or become miserable and weak.
Fight for the right to freedom, or succumb to being enslaved,
Act against our conscience or stand up for what is right,
Fall into self-pity and despair, or fight with the courage of
        the brave,
Knowing that, if we do not make a choice, circumstance will
        devise our fate.

OF HUMAN NATURE

There is a school we must all attend, and that is the school of
        Human Nature,
Where lessons are taught and lessons are learned, where we
Sometimes make mistakes and sometimes beat the odds, in those
Experiences we choose to pursue or in those that seek to find us.
The circumstances we encounter, the hidden agendas, the earthly
        travelers we meet along the way,
Are all subjects of the grade we achieve, in how wisely we live
        our lives,
In surmounting the challenges and overcoming the odds, of all that
        might come our way.

There are so many factions in our human being, when our human
        persona is all laid bare,
A cast of characters we all are, each of us playing out a role with
        our emotions running wild,
And in our interaction with one another, we will show the true colors
        of who and what we are.
We will encounter the human paradox, the walking chameleon,
Who shows one side of his face to the world, while another side lurks
        in the shadows
Known only behind closed doors or to those of his camaraderie.

We will always meet the critics, the Mr. and Miss know-it-all on every
Topic, and of course the gossipmongers whose tongues never skip a beat
As they survey, scan and scrutinize everything that meet their eyes.
In the mirror of their minds, live the arrogant, the ever loving narcissist
All filled up with their self-ego and self-importance, trying hard to
Convince themselves, that they stand one rung higher on life's ladder
        overlooking the rest of us.
Then there are the idlers content to lazily watch life pass them by,
Living in their own world of make-believe, always studying how to
        get over and get by.

They stand next in line to the moochers who hang on for a free ride,
Happy to take out of life whatever he or she can, at the expense of
        someone else.

Along life's passing parade are the human barters, who trade their
        bodies for the best offer they can get,
They will use all the tricks of their trade to lure, entice and connive
Even though, unknown to them or perhaps uncaring, the danger
        of predators who see them as an easy prey.
Into this universal arena, walks the ever vigilant users, whose game it is
To cheat and lie or to con and scam whenever they can, as they seek
        to make their mark.
They will make false promises while feigning sincerity, which they never
        mean to keep,
As they create every means they can find to assure you to believe in them
        and keep you satisfied.

Worst of all are the controlling abusers who feel they must always be
        in charge
Hiding their own insecurities by lashing out on others, reveling in their
        tyranny to create fear one way or another.
Cowards who cannot admit to their own faults and instead always
        seeking to blame someone else.
They will advance step by step going easily from words of charm, to
        striking out with great force and harm.
The Instigator is anywhere and everywhere, at the most inopportune time,
Lays in waiting somewhere, and even in the most crowded circle will try to
Stir up the moment with some outlandish remark, or behavior, or resurrect
Old forgotten tales, if only to be noticed, even if it is done with humor,
        or embarrassment to another.

Here comes the braggart, the showpiece of the moment, with his obnoxious
        manner.
He could have everything he says, or nothing at all, yet will try to convince
Whoever will listen, that he is some kind of prize catch, in his loud way,
        he will always crave attention.
We will see m any smooth faces, with looks that seem so refined, but alas
        whose manners spell words like "crude" and "coarse".

The Thrill-seekers like living life on the edge, hinging one step away
in their gamble with life and death
Addicted to whatever turns them on, taking a fast treadmill all the way
for their ride.
Yes, this is a school of Human Nature where lessons are taught and lessons
are learned,
Among the good and noble, the high and low, the bright and the
beautiful and the meek and merciful,
There will always be the givers and takers of this great University.

TRUE FRIENDSHIP-A GIFT OF LOVE

Today I looked at you and realized just how lucky I have
　　　　　been,
You not only share a part of my life, but you're the best
　　　　　friend I ever had.
You have been there when I needed you, throughout life's
　　　　　ups and downs,
You made me see blue skies through clouds of grey, often
　　　　　encouraging me in every way.

I reflect on the gifts you brought to my life, over all the
　　　　　years gone by,
And the littlest of things which mean so much, because
　　　　　you are a true friend of mine.
I thank my lucky stars for knowing you, and for moments
　　　　　we enjoyed together,
I cherish the ways you brightened up my life, as we looked
　　　　　at the world together,
And remember the times you were a tower of strength on
　　　　　my roads of triumph and defeat.

I thank you for clearing the cobwebs from my mind when I
　　　　　couldn't see clearly to choose,
For helping me hang on to my self-confidence when hope
　　　　　seemed futile to me.
Most of all, for making me see, what loyalty in a true friend
　　　　　can mean.
As I look into the mirror of my mind, the word "Love" stands
　　　　　out most clearly,
And so I feel I must take this time to say, you are always
　　　　　thought of, loved and appreciated,
For friendships like ours that linger through a lifetime, comes
　　　　　around just once in a while.

MIXED EMOTIONS

How can we explain the mind, and the mixed emotions
          we all have of every kind.
How can we explain the mistakes we all make, some
Of which, will never find reason enough to compensate.
How can we explain words we held back that we should
          have said,
Those words which now lay with a thousand regrets
          spinning around inside our head.

How do we express the love we selfishly held in reserve,
The love for someone whom we knew, it was so richly
          deserved.
Why do we allow time to snatch away someone from
          our sight,
Then wish we could move heaven and earth to make
          things right.
And why, do we hold back tears, that in hurt and
          sorrow we should have shed,
By bottling them up inside our heart instead.

Why do we assume things about others for which we
          have no basis
By simply looking at them or trying to read their faces.
Why do we look at others to make us happy, then blame
          them for what we cannot find,
Before we realize, that by our own choices, we bring the
          gift of happiness around.

Why do we constantly put people on a pedestal convincing
          ourselves they are beyond any flaw,
And only seem to realize when they fall out of our grace,
That they are just as human as all of within the human race.
Oh, those mixed emotions, that always seem to come into
          play,
Often determines the pain or joy we feel, on the path to our destiny.

OLD FRIENDS

Old friends are like comfortable old shoes,
The kind you feel at home in, and love, and can
        wear around all day.
There is a coziness and familiarity with them,
And an understanding you both know,
All there is to know about each other, and it
        feels good.

Old friends are like an oasis, to which you
Constantly resort, and they know you inside out.
They know when you feel on top of the world,
They sense when you are down and blue,
They know what to expect of you, and how to give
        and take with you,
And just when to give a push to steer you right.

Old friends are vintage stuff, rare and valuable.
Withstanding time like carved and polished wood,
Whose beauty belies its age and linger in our minds,
Forever precious and appealing, and so they carry
        on with us,
Truly faithful and well meaning.

Old friends know that from time to time, they will
        disagree with you,
And they will let you know with all due respect, just
        what is on their minds,
And if you decide their opinion, you do not wish
        to hear,
Deep down you know it is said, because they really care.

Old friends are there when you need them, always a
Part of, and caught up, into the life you are leading.
Their eyes are the mirror through which you might see,
      all that you are reflecting,
And no matter what life hands you on your journey
      day after day,
They are always in your corner or waiting, in the wings
      along the way,

Old friends cannot be bought or sold, they are a treasure
      beyond compare,
In times of good fortune or travail, their love will shine
      through strong,
And should you fall, they will pick you up, and help you
      carry on.
What is the price of friendship such as this? the answer
      will always be,
One no gold in the world could buy, for it is a priceless
      commodity.

PART II

Slices of life
Vignettes A thru Y

"Seasons show us life must change, when leaves fall off
trees in Autumn yet find new birth again in Spring"

PART II

SLICES OF LIFE – VIGNETTES (A through Y)

"Anger, Brutality, Change, Children, Compassion, Courage, Despair, Domestic Abuse, Devotion, Divorce, Disloyalty, Emotions, Encouragement, Fear, Friendship, Faith, Family, Greed, Gratitude, Generosity, Good Samaritan, Humor, Happiness, Intuition, Indulgence, Innocence, Jealousy, Kindness, Loneliness, Life, Leisure, Life Choices, Love, Marriage, Men, Obsession, Optimism, Pessimism, Peace, Perseverance, Prisoner, Retreat, Racism, Respect, Success, Self-Discovery, Secrets, Self-Esteem, Sorrow, Tranquility, Talk, Talent, Vindictiveness, Women, Youth."

REFLECTIONS THROUGH AN HOURGLASS

Anger: Repressed anger is a dangerous commodity. It can harbor a walking time bomb, it can tee off without the slightest provocation and considers a mere word or gesture a threat. It can cause harm and pain. It never just fade away, like anything else, the cause must be examined, addressed and resolved. It needs help in the most urgent way.

Brutality: Acts that defy human reasoning. Look at the bully, the tyrant, the indifferent one, whose satisfaction to make oneself appear powerful, serves himself or herself by intimidation or trying to control others in a brutish way. Within them is an ocean of turbulence, capped by waves of disharmony always waiting to be unleashed on someone or society at large. Observe their tone of voice, watch their strides and heed their body language. Somewhere along the way their companions will be anger, arrogance, aloofness or narcissism.

Change: "Time marches on and so must we"(Anon).
When the light goes out on one rung of Life's ladder, and it signals the end of a road, keep climbing. Climb in whatever way you can. Climb with that long awaited trip, climb by capturing nature on canvas, climb by enriching your knowledge, climb into a new way of life, but keep on climbing, for the wheel of life never stops turning.

Children: "And a little child shall lead them"(The Bible)
Children are a light in the world. For in their curiosity and exploration of the Universe, they are learning, growing and questioning our evolvement and, by so doing they challenge us to prove ourselves worthy of their being.

Compassion: A beautiful quality that too few people cultivate today. The ability to feel empathy for others. It is a matter of heart and soul.

Courage: Courage is the most amazing thing, for it can suddenly surprise us. It can leap out of the least courageous heart as it fights bravely within another.

Despair: So life has given you a kick or two, and maybe those we love don't always do by us as they ought to do, but life has its ups and downs and broken promises too, but does life stand still? Not a chance of it. The weather will still change, the seasons will still move one to another, days are still numbered and time keeps ticking away. Circumstances are necessary for change and change is essential to our finding new paths.

Domestic Abuse: It is physically scarring, emotionally draining and verbally the words cut to the core of your being. Sexually it can cause all kinds of chaos in your life. Imagine life like a kaleidoscope, you will keep on seeing the same picture, unless you move away from it to change the pattern.

Devotion: Oh how it cares, it nurtures, it hovers, it pursues. It is dedicated, but it can also be sacrificial. Learn how to balance it. Give yourself a breath of fresh air, and life will be beautiful all over again.

Divorce; The farewell to a chapter of our lives. Time heals and time discovers, and we will discover the next chapter of our lives through something or someone else Divorce like marriage is a moment in time, it doesn't come with a written guarantee. The most important thing is that we learn something of importance from each experience we are privileged to have.

Disloyalty: The greatest betrayal when it comes from those we love and trust the most. It not only hurts, it wounds, and if you have never learned how to forgive and move on with your life, this is the opportunity. For, if you cannot, the wound will keep erupting and erupting over again in your mind. Let it go!

Emotions: Coldness, Indifference and Hate are captives of a heart empty of love. In its hollow chambers the only echo it hears are its own. It has to be taught all over again a new way to the joys of living.

Encouragement: Sweet, sweet refreshment when it is needed most, for it gives new life. It is rejuvenation for it gives purpose to our lives and can start possibilities in us that lead to a new lease on life.

Fear: Who among us can say they haven't known fear of something or someone, at sometime. It is a natural part of our mortality, and when it rears its head, it either absorbs our minds, plays with our hearts, or ties our stomach in knots. To combat fear we must weigh its strength against us like an enemy, then decide how best to fight it, or it will engulf us.

Friendship; True friendship is that loyal bond of understanding between hearts, each with its own dreams, each with its own destiny, yet always sharing in a meeting of the minds.

Faith: How many times have we told faith goodbye and shrink into the shadows of our own desperation, only to realize it is the most essential lifeline we have to succeed at anything.

Family: The guardians in our earthly arena. We all command the attention of each other in one way or another, and what a prize package we are. We come in all different sizes, shapes and colors. Then we have the good one, the bad one, the off-the wall one, the living on the edge one, and the I can't stand your ways one. Yet, in the bond of kinship, we keep on loving one another. Phew ! all in a day's work.

Greed: It shows itself so conspicuously. It is brazen, it is demanding, it is unending. it is all consuming, all the way to the end of its road. It can bring all kinds of trouble. Walk away from it.

Gratitude: Will always show itself in appreciation, graciousness and humble grace.

Generosity: It has a nature all its own. Sometimes it is spontaneous, Sometimes constant, for it has a heart larger than life.

Good Samaritan: People are not known or remembered just for who they are, but by their deeds. And so, the unsung heroes of our time, the everyday Jack or Jill that goes beyond the call of duty, the Angels in disguise who give that helping hand when needed, or rises to that unexpected moment, is the Good Samaritan we all could be.

Humor: It is the bridge between our sanity and going over the edge. It is the interlude in our chaotic world that allows us to laugh at ourselves, see the world how we want to and remind ourselves not to take life too seriously.

Happiness: It is a kind of euphoric contentment. It is arriving at that place in which mind, body and soul connect if even for a brief space in time to feel totally at peace with itself and the world.

Intuition: It is a presentiment of mind, a knowing, a hunch, a gut feeling, a guiding spirit. However it might impress itself upon you, and it's there when you need it, heed it.

Indulgence; A sweet fruit that can turn bitter when its roots are found in selfishness and ingratitude. Sadly it is often the reward for not shaping a tree before it is bent, to coin a biblical phrase − "sparing the rod and spoiling the child" − a little discipline never hurts

Innocence: I found its purest essence in a baby's eyes, a baby's trusting grasp, a baby's honest smile.

Jealousy: It begins like a small flame, flickering endlessly back and forth until it launches itself into a steady flame burning brighter all the while, as one's objective seem unattainable. If one's wish is out of reach or desires seem threatened by another, or there is a feeling of being unloved or insecure. It could be in a relationship, in family ties, in sibling rivalry, in interaction with acquaintances. It could arise over the smallest of things, that seem insignificant to someone else. Whenever or however it rears its head, pay attention to it, for it can be spiteful, and create havoc. Decide how best to handle it, but know that it is deep-rooted from something.

Kindness: An understanding heart, a gentle hand, and a loving smile will always leave its imprint on your mind.

Loneliness: It can creep up on you like a fog, and surround you, blotting out whatever is on the outside of it The world is full of many people who have had their share of life's pitfalls, but who have decided that looking in on life, can in no way compare to being a part of it.

Life: To think that the world is passing us by unseen is not a singular idea. In one instant we live with thoughts of our forgotten existence and are transported back to the reality that we have to make up for lost time. Life is for living.

Leisure: Take time amid the rushing current that life is to enjoy, enjoy, enjoy, your life. For it is not just built upon the fortunes to which we aspire, but we will find that as we go through life's twists and turns, it will be the simple pleasures we have allowed ourselves that will burn most brightly in our minds and sustain us.

Life Choices: Life is all about choices and we have the right to choose what we desire our life to be. Whatever we might do, there will always be circumstances that face us and consequences good and bad that will surface around us. The thing to remember is no life, no matter how perfect a life it might seem, it will still know its darkest hour yet can still embrace a shining dawn.

Love: Unconditional love is non-judgmental. It is forever cognizant of human imperfections It doesn't seeks to blame or constantly find fault. It understands how to put itself in another's shoe, for it rides upon a wind called "understanding."

Marriage: Promises, Promises — In sickness or in health, for richer or poorer, for better or for worse. Let us think carefully when we make that vow, for if we cannot mean what we are saying, somewhere down the line when circumstances demand it of us, unless we are committed to the promise we make, we will not rise to the occasion. The moment can be a fairytale, but living it is real.

Men: Young men look around you at our society and footsteps of the past to change the tide of the times. Let the word "Dad" live out the meaning of what it is supposed to be. Be there when your children need you, let them know they are loved. Nurture understand and care them, for today is the beginning of the rest of their lives. To be remembered by them, you must stand up to what life asks of you as a Dad and be counted. Always keep in mind that today's deeds reap tomorrow's reward.

Obsession: Self-control thrown through the window. A refusal to see that balance is not in the measure of the life you lead. For there is no measure in extremes and it usually takes a side-trip to disillusion when the ultimate desire sought is not achieved. Passion is good but when it becomes a consuming preoccupation we are skating on thin ice.

Optimism: The optimist signifies "Hope". He secretly knows that as day follows night, out of the ashes of despair, like a Phoenix rising, Hope can materialize.

Pessimism: The pessimist sees a dark road with shadows lurking around every corner. It is always the rain coming down instead of the rainbow that might appear. It is always the cloudy day, instead of the sun coming out. Lighten up! Let the sunshine in.

Peace: An honored guest in any home. She enters softly, speaks gently, and touches the hearts of all she encounters.

Perseverance: The art of perseverance is a test of human endurance. For, it can frustrate your mind, will make you throw your hands up into the air, and cause an all out war with your emotions. But, if you can hold out long enough for any worthwhile cause, things that looked unshakeable at first, will begin to shift or open up, taking you completely by surprise.

Prisoner: There are all kinds of prisoners in the world. Prisoners caught in a web of circumstances, prisoners addicted to someone or something, prisoners locked away because of being misguided or mis-directed, or through some grievous mistake of their own. Whatever the circumstance might have been, every life comes to a crossroad at some point where you must consider what your destination must be. Think hard and think carefully then, for that is the point where you must decide where change will have its way with you, or you will be resigned to repeating old habits, and paying the same old dues.

Respect: Paying homage where it is due and learning how to earn it too. A quality of mind that cannot be bought. Like charity it begins at home. A manner of speaking, a manner of respecting another's rights and property, a manner of addressing someone, a manner of treating someone the way we would all like to be treated. The reward it brings could be surprising.

Racism: The world is a melting pot of nations yet it is constantly at war with itself. How do we change the world? We cannot reverse the actions of the past, or turn back the hands of time, we can only change ourselves and how we look at the world, at life and at others. If we should remember how many times we wished we were spoken to or treated with the respect we deserved, we would extend the same courtesy to others. If we could look at our own heritage, we would find that through our own ancestors we have channeled through many countries within our own lineage, and despite our ethnic differences we are still linked in a continuous human chain of a recurring cycle. We are born, we live, we think, we feel, and eventually we die. It doesn't seem that we are that much different., than the different circumstances in which we are born, the different lives we choose to lead or the different life we are able to afford ourselves.

Retreat: The oasis on our journey. It is spiritual enrichment for a spirit in need of enlightenment, seeking solace with its soul. Some of us meditate, some of us pray, some of us turn inward to the sanctuary of our inner being. However we might retreat to find our consolation, our conscious being will awake revitalized and renewed, with new thoughts, aspirations, hopes and visions.

Success: Success is not attained by now and then, one of these days, or sooner or later. It is a steady stream of extraordinary willpower focused upon a particular goal, that gives you the determination to seek out all the necessary means, to achieve your ultimate end.

Self-Discovery: Who are you? You are a wonderful creation of God's universe. You are no less than anyone else regardless of being rich or poor or despite your incapability. You are here to write your history in Life's Times, and make it a good one. You can only be as good as you believe yourself to be, or as great as you desire to be. You must first look within yourself and discover your strength and weaknesses to know what you are working with. You cannot let anyone dismiss your dreams because they cannot believe in you. You alone know what you can do, and the dreams you have, honor them and discover yourself. You might surprise yourself at the greatness that lies within you.

Secrets: How real are our lives when we smile at the world while hiding in a corner of our minds, "some secret past"? For the tide of the ocean to flow in, it must flow out, or it will overflow its bank. Take heed from the tide, and decide whether you will flow with the tide of life or continually struggle against it. A clean heart and a clear mind can work wonders.

Self-Esteem: It is confidence in yourself, a feeling of well being and good morale. The courage to know you can go after what you believe in and succeed at it. It is knowing you are worth something and believing it against all odds.

Sorrow: It touches everyone's path in some way, for it is a turn along the highway of life's journey, one which we can never quite come to terms with, but have to accept and learn how to move on. The reality is it is an inevitable destination for us all. But while we are still on the journey we must take comfort that the spirit of that loved one is very much alive in spirit, in our hearts and around us. We all have a purpose, a beginning and an end. Our goal is to find our mission for this life's journey, know the meaning of it and pursue it to its fullest.

Tranquility: There is a kind of stillness so awe-inspiring that if you ever experience it you never forget it. I knew such stillness once, on a summer day in the heart of the California mountains. Away from the noise and sounds of city life, everything seemed suspended in a frozen moment. Time seemed to stand still and in its brief repose, the overpowering stillness of the summer day was only broken by the cawing of a crow. In the madness of city life, this kind of stillness escapes us. Once in a while let your spirit enjoy this kind of solitude, it is a world of its own, within a world.

Talk: Talk! Talk! Talk! We talk to others and others talk back to us. The gift of speech can be a powerful tool in the right hands, a verbally harmful tool in the wrong hands and a disturbing tool in the hands of the indecisive. The right hands can elevate and empower, the wrong hands can intimidate and strip away layer by layer to the core of the human spirit. Indecisiveness is parlayed in an endless banter of words that become like a jigsaw, never seeming to come together, leaving behind only confusion or distress, meaning nothing of consequence. Think before you talk, and ask yourself, what kind of message am I conveying?

Talent: It is that knowing voice inside of you that makes you know you can do something even if others think you can't. It is the pulse of your desires constantly throbbing or tugging at your heartstrings to remind you it's waiting in the wings to burst upon the world. Set it free!

Vindictiveness: What fury, what vengeance, meanspirited and spiteful people can be a dangerous hazard for they will leap first and look after at the damage they have caused. In their moment of spite, they will not consider nor realize the recriminations of their actions until its over. Do yourself a favor and avoid them if you can.

Women: We are mothers, daughters, sisters, grandmothers, aunts, nieces, cousins, wives and lovers. We are doctors, lawyers, housewives. We are nurturers and sometimes sole providers, we are givers and takers. We are here, and there and everywhere, but we are on the move. Women of the 21st century, young, old or in-between, are coming into their own recognition, that they can achieve anything if they put their mind to it. Women have a history of being held back, looked over, overlooked, abandoned, abused, repressed, but we are still on the move. Today more than ever we are making long strides, taking risks and reaching up and out towards all we aspire to be-no holds barred. The road might still be rocky, the challenges sometimes beyond our control, but lookout when you hear us coming, for we are still on the move . . . . Hello?

Youth: An old man digs into the past to find the boy he was. A young man climbs into the future, to discover the man he wants to be. An old woman looks into the mirror to find traces of the girl she used to be. A girl looks into the mirror to see how quickly she's changing into the woman she longs to be. Life is a paradox

PART III

Along life's Avenues
Poetic Verses

"All around the world let kindness be a beacon of Hope"

It's a New Day

The days might sometimes seem too long, and the nights
        stretch endlessly on,
But the world as we know it, will keep on turning,
And each of us, immersed in our own thoughts or action
        will survive and keep on going.
The pattern of life will always be the same – "give and take."
For life will take us through the cycles of up and down,
        back and forth, good and bad.
Losing and winning, and missing the boat at times, and,
Out of the blue surprise us with something we desire.

The seasons change and so must we, looking at life
Through different lens, to discover what life is showing us –
The rain falls, yet the sun always filters through.
The storm rages, yet it leaves a calm behind.
The ocean tides go out but they must come in.
The sun goes down each evening, but rises again to
        greet a new day.

The truth is, this is the story of life, regardless of whatever
        avenues we find ourselves upon.
Simply put, life is saying to us, our trials and errors are
        only for a season.
Change is the order of the day, and it will come to us in
        its own way.
Giving us the choice to contemplate how to embrace each
        new direction.
Knowing that when we understand the order of the Universe,
We leave the door open for miracles to happen.

MAKING THE WORLD A BETTER PLACE

As I looked out at the world today wondering how we could
         make it better,
I realized what it needed most of all, was locked away inside
         of us,
Deep within the recess of our minds, we had filed away,
         brotherly love and trust.

We had allowed ourselves to become wrapped up, into the web
         of just our daily lives,
Content to come and go, in an unending assembly line, intent
         on only our own affairs,
Many of us bent on achieving only our own desires, as if we were
Caught in a race with time, to capture our own utopia.

Where and when we should ask ourselves, did we begin losing
         sight,
Of the reality and purpose of our very dispensable life.
Was it, as civilization moved us out of the avenues of yesteryear?
Was it then, it robbed us, of the simple joys of kindness that we
         all used to know and share?
Today super technology, authority and power, overwhelms us here
         and there,
And, enamored with all of this, we ceased to understand or care.

Amazing how we forget human frailties that are common in us all,
When we are quick to condemn human qualities in others, of which
         we think they seem to fall short,
But, who among us have not felt our own human stirrings of weakness
         within our own mind,
Knowing we only suppressed our urge to act on it, by the grace of God,
         and the greatest determination we could find.

Upon Love and Kindness no one can ever put a price, for it sends its
own message as it works its miracle.
Love has made strong men weaken and weaker men become strong,
Kindness has lifted up the downtrodden when their road seem far
too long,
Loving words have reassured someone feeling lonely or out of place,
Kindness has eased many fears and put a smile upon someone's face.

Our lives are all too brief an interlude in this endless sea of time
And as travelers together, our roads will cross in some way, some
time and some place.
Life is not all coming and going but our acts and deeds exchanged
along the way,
That adds up from sunrise to sunset as we rise to greet the dawn
of each new day.
We cannot and must not let our chance to make a difference in the world
just slip away,
And let new promises dissolve, that we could have given to some
life that have gone astray,
Love is a universal word, spoken everywhere, always breaking down
barriers,
And, crossing bridges, because it simply says, "I care."

Today someone's life could be turned around because of one good deed,
Whether it's a helping hand to a friend, or neighbor or stranger in a
moment of need,
And justice dispensed with some advice and compassion, could mean
A straighter road for someone feeling forgotten and confused, if we could
Only try looking at the distance, they have walked in their shoes.
We are all subjects of the Universe, that we must bear in mind,
That even if the earthly passions we strive for and possessions we amass
becomes our driving force,
They still belong to the waves of circumstances we might endure and
our rendezvous with time.
For when we can see clearly through the mist and maze of life, they
are earthly souvenirs,

A record of things we liked, the places we visited, whom and what
we loved.
But our true legacy to our life and times, wont lie in just ornaments
no matter how beautiful they might seem
It will shine out in acts and deeds, lives touched, lives changed by us,
That is the legacy that will speak to the world and say- "This is the
way I lived my life, and the essence of who I was."

MUSICIANS

He is alive whose soul has found its joy, in music's
            mystical ways,
She can capture even the rebel, running wild and free,
            seducing him effortlessly.
Music is the divine mistress, she will command, she
            will compel,
That he gives deep out of his soul, all that he can give.

So, he plays his guitar to a fevered pitch, his body trembling
            with emotion,
Every fiber of his being, in tune with his melody,
And, in that capsule of time, nothing else will belong, when
 His music and his soul become joined as one.

The piano man plays on and on, tinkling away on the ivories,
Fascinating all with his impromptu style, in his own inimitable
            way,
Letting his heart and mind succumb to just being a captive
            of music's old sweet way.

Then the drummer comes in swift and strong, rapping out her
Beats with a frenzy on the drums, drums, drums,
In rhythm to the left, in rhythm to the right, with a clash of brass
Echoing and echoing, till it fades away at last., but for that brief
            moment, she knows,
Music has touched a part of heaven, deep into her heart, that only
            her soul could know.

And, if someday we should listen carefully, to the strains of a
            symphony,
From the violin sweet, to a cello and flute, we will understand,
Why these masters of their art, are willing subjects of music's
            spell.
For within their hearts and their souls, her divine magic dwells.

THE DANCER

She stands like a vision in the night,
In raiments of shimmering gold and white,
Poised with her hands above her head, her
Presence commands, no words need to be said.
Slowly her body sways with passion and heat,
Gently her feet taps out the rhythmic beat,
Then, as if someone suddenly struck the right
      key,
With a frenzy of motion, she is lost in rapture
      and glory.

Her costume casts little prisms of light, as she
      swirled,
First to the left, then to the right, like a most
      graceful bird in flight
She mesmerized, she dazzled, she captured the
      night,
She had the audience in the palm of her hand,
      holding them spellbound.
Before she bowed, there wasn't a sound,
Then, just thunderous applause, and Encore! Encore!

AND SO LIFE IS

Life is a moment of truth, an awakening of the
     soul,
The birth of a new dawn, the sunset signaling day
     is gone,
It is one moment that will stand out in a lifetime
     forever, as unequaled and unmatched,
And so life is.

Life is magic, it is surprises, it is down and out,
     it is roundabout.
It is joy in one measure, sorrow in another,
It is defeat and it is triumph, it is courage in its
     finest hour,
It is that still small voice that echoes in our ear
     making us wonder,
And so life is.

Life is serenity and hope and forgiveness, emotions
     we all share,
It is the changing of the seasons, the ebb and flow
     of ocean tides,
It is the course we chart upon this journey, roads
     we choose along the way,
It is the beauty of Mother Nature, the kindness to
     us by Father Time,
And so life is.

Life is the love and friendship that find us, and
the many ties that bind us,
Dreams and visions to remind us, of all that we
can be,
It is the unguarded moment, that shows us who
and what we are,
It is the light we cast upon the world, amid our
changing times,
All avenues along our way,
And so life is.

LOVE

Love can gradually rise, degree by degree, until it
    is a sublime feeling,
Then like waves lashing to a crescendo as they rise
    and fall into the sea,
It will leap out of the heart like a captive set free.
Love can be faithful and constant as the sun,
Never ceasing, though wavering, it will never run.
Love such as this, can be accepting of faults and
    forgiving,
Even when its patience is tried, it will still shine
    and keep on giving.

Love will stoop to please, and to communicate
    will bend.
Love can stand strong like the mighty oak, and
    endure like the evergreen,
It can survive through age and time, and will
    be forever seen.
Love, the greatest human emotion, can spellbind us.
And, as wise as we may be, it is a subject of the
    heart,
When the heart rules, we will turn our head aside.
And without question, succumb to our feeling,
    and simply close our eyes.
When the head rules, we will tap into our minds
    and walk in step with reason.

IDEAS

Ideas, Ideas, Ideas, they come from the break of dawn, throughout
the day, even in the midnight hour.
They will hammer in our minds until we take notice, or linger around,
getting at us here and there,
Or hit us like a bolt of lightning, or nag at us until we decide we
must lend an ear
To those ideas that remain uninvited, yet riveted in our thoughts, daring
us to take a leap of faith,
Or driving us towards the arms of progress, but most of all making sure
we will respond.

Ideas put into practice have fostered great inventions, or made radical
change,
Ideas have saved lives, courted peace, prevented disaster, commanded
the course of history,
They have overcome injustice, broke down barriers, and made break-
throughs in life,
The possibilities of which would have gone unseen, if it were not for
Someone, or for the many others, working in unison to put purpose
To their insight for the good of another or for the advancement of
humanity.

What good are ideas that lay dormant in our minds, ideas that we know
Lay on our doorstep, waiting to be harnessed by us and spun into
something worthwhile.
Ideas that would enable us to see for ourselves a new way or a new day
Or alternatives to matters that besiege us, or to things that cause us to
sit up and pay attention.
Where would we be without ideas – those thoughts that pour forth from
our hearts and minds,
Thoughts which set our lives on a course that gives us a life changing
experience,
Whether it challenges us to crusade for the rights of others or to discover
Our own selves and the value of who we are, or our own true self-worth.

Ideas are without a doubt, a spark of light, sometimes even a flash of
Inspiration and a continuous thread of Hope, and always a lifeline for us
      to carry on.
Ideas have taken many people from need and want to rise up and astound
      the world
And, even surprise themselves of the greatness within them and the power
      to persevere, conquer and triumph.
Ideas have bolstered the strength of men and women through the darkest
Storm, opening up a whole new world to many and overturning tragedy
      and giving rise to hope.
Ideas have shown others that nothing, however difficult it might seem, is
      impossible if they believe in an idea,
Knowing that once it takes root, it can open all kinds of doors, and make
Lives that once felt useless and hopeless, sprout new wings and amaze
      us all.

Ideas, ideas, Ideas, contemplate them all, think where they might lead,
      and what is their worth in time.
Exchange ideas, for each one of us can learn something we never knew
      before,
And mutual endeavors, sometimes bring about great rewards we never
      expected,
Today my friend, you might feel you are down on your luck, but ideas
      are born every day.
Put your imagination to work, think of what you are good at doing and
      how you can improve that skill or craft,
And, when that bright idea comes along or that offer comes your way
that fate intended, you just might get real "Lucky".

LISTEN

Listen is a word, most of us seldom wish to hear,
Even while someone is shouting it at us, we often
   turn a deaf ear.
It's not because we really do not care,
But may be preoccupied, or simply unaware, that
   all that is being asked of us
Is one moment of our time, to listen to someone
   who, only needs to ease their mind.

The call could be from a friend in need, whose
Signal somehow, we just failed to heed, or maybe
From a loved one see-sawing on dangerous ground,
Frantically, screaming, "Listen" I am just one step
   away from jumping off a ledge.
Yet the signs were all around us like flags waving
   in our face,
All pushed aside by claims we were too busy, to be
   the true friend or parent we should be.

Later on we might wonder what they might have said,
Or perhaps in some way, we could have eased their
   burden, or changed the life they led.
In sparing a little time to listen, we could help someone
   to cope,
In responding to someone's call we could salvage
   shattered hope.
In cultivating the art of listening, we could learn
   something new,
For many times things pass us by, pass by because
   we hear so few.

LOVE ME NOW

Love me now for life is forever a spinning wheel of
Entrance and exits, twists and turns, highways and detours.
Sweet love can turn sour, as much as it can be long or
      short-lived.
Love can be touching one life with its own brand of sweet
      perfume
While it is busily tunneling through another life, leaving
      only heartbreak behind.
Love can be as constant as it can be contrary, and can be
      prudent as it can be confounding,
And, if we allow ourselves to contemplate the whys and
      wherefore of it all,
We will find love has moved on, away from us, or left us
      behind,
To linger on the precipice of hopeful tomorrows, searching
      for,
The perfect, the ideal, the one in a million, that seemingly
      eludes us, so love me now.
For, whatever your imperfections might be, to love you in
      return will be my folly,
For in the span of my lifetime, I alone will have to ask myself
If this whim of mine, this flight of fancy was worth the time
      we stayed together.
Once in a lifetime or maybe twice if luck smiles upon us, life
      opens a door of chance,
And we all must decide whether to embrace someone new or
      hold on to old habits and old ways,
This is where we should ask ourselves the question, to whom
      do we say "Love me now."
Or we will find ourselves on a continuous merry-go-round
      asking what if, maybe, and wondering.

PASSION

Passion, what is the secret of your power?
What magic potion did you conjure up that still weaves
        its spell throughout the ages,
To make us all captives of the heart? Was it in one look,
One smile, one alluring glance, that we are caught like
        a spider in your web?

O, foolish Passion, you are like bittersweet wine,
First, hot, then warm, then hot again, then warm,
Off and on again, then cold, as cold as ice can be, when
        passion dies.
Where is the laughter we used to hear?
It's just an echo now of a time we used to share.

And Passion, what happened to the promises we vowed
        to keep
And all the rosy dreams we planned together?
All blown away on the wind now, light as a feather.
Do you remember all those places we have been,
And the world without end, we swear we would stay in?

O, cruel Passion how fickle is your game, as you reach
        out in pursuit, time and time again.
You are a conjurer of sweet words in your quest for
        delight,
Painting visions of beauty to lovers, here and there in the
        night.
Yet, you will not care, when you move on, for betrayed
Hearts or broken dreams you leave behind, so unkind, when
        passion dies.

And Passion, should you meet again a lost romance, somewhere
    unexpected,
You would be as a stranger caught in an awkward moment, no
    longer sure of what to do or say,
Forgetting all that used to be, you would only acknowledge that
    lover, as cold as only ice can be when passion dies.
For all there was, all you will see are, dying embers and cold ashes
    of some kind of love that used to be.

MOTHERHOOD

Mother, Mamma Mia, Mi Madre, Ma Mere, in any language says it all,
She is the beginning of the essence of who we are, and our benefactor
    to our introduction into the world.
The one in whose body we are conceived, the one person that will nurture,
Or if not, will haunt our mind in some way until we make our final bow.
Our birth sets in motion, the course of a life whose foundation to flourish,
Will depend on the roots we inherit, and the environment we will live in.
The nurturing or neglect we receive, the care and devotion of a mother or
    father and grandparent will carry its weight, but
The actions of our life bearer, whether good or bad, will leave its imprint
    on our heart and mind forever.

The bonds of a mother and child are special, and when it is built on love
    and trust for each other, it is timeless and infinite
However the joys of motherhood or mother and child reunion are not
    always what it should be, and here is where,
The realities of life opens up to us, the good, the bad, and complexities
    of motherhood.
For, mothers will always observe each other and question themselves
Why the offspring of one might excel in matters of behavior, focus and
    in achieving goals,
While their own child given the same set of opportunities turn in an
    opposing direction.

Other mothers will see children with far less in life and greater adversity
    scale great heights, and,
Other children surrounded with all the material advances for a successful
    life be ungrateful and uncaring.
The question always is – how, when and why do our children find
    themselves in situations that leave parents asking,
How did this all come about? That is when you will look back in your
Memory bank and find little things you overlooked or long ago should
Have corrected, and retrace your steps to find what has brought
    this dilemma home to Mother.

Sometimes it begins when we start treating children like little adults,
When we impose upon them the burden of taking on a parental role and
forget that children still need time to be a child,
At other times we allow John or Jane to act like they are the parents,
and Mother is the child, to be told what to do.
A total role reversal of children dictating to parents and speaking to
them in the most despicable way, and,
Mothers and Fathers, giving up on their children and deciding there is
nothing they can do about them.
Children being allowed to cut into their parents adult discussions without
being told it's not proper to do so.
Young children and teenagers on the streets, coming and going all
hours of the night, without any curfews.
Children leaving their homes, dressed in all kinds of revealing clothing
or immodest attire, without a word said to them,
Children coming home talking about dating, at too young an age, and
feeling they have the okay to do so.

There are parent s giving too much to their children in order to win their
affection, with no thought to their own self,
And, children demanding too much of their parents, oblivious to the
sacrifices that are being made for them.
Children who, left to their own devices usually find themselves in all
kinds of trouble, which will land at Mother's feet.
Of course, there is a flip side to everything and there are parents who
do the best they can in their circumstances, and,
Their children whether rich or poor, rise above the crowd because of
Parents who teach them that morals, values and principles in life, are
still the main ingredients of a life well worth living.

Mothers who love your children until you are blind to their faults,
Whose hackles rise up when your attention is called to their lack
of self-control or behavior – wake up!
Often, their cry for help in acting out often goes unanswered by those
they need the most.
When they grow up, they will not thank you for giving them their way,
Instead they will say you never communicated with them by listening
to them or even trying to understand.

Together you would make great strides in resolving their problem or
      seeking help for them.

For those mothers who have neglected their children, cast them aside
Deprived them of the nurturing love every child you bring into the
      world should have,
You have left them feeling abandoned and alienated and they will feel
Haunted by memories about you that time will never fade, and a life
That will demand more of them than most can ever handle — Where
      is your conscience? Time alone will have that answer.
Its never too late to reach out and make right where your life went wrong.
Mother, Mamma Mia, Mi Madre, Ma Mere, in any language says it all.

The Clock

Tick-tock, Tick-tock, the clock on the wall says it all.
For it reminds us that we are time travelers, it makes us
      realize if we stop and think,
That every event in our lives have taken place, in those
Minutes and hours, we take for granted every day.
Night and day, good and bad, are all tallied into that fleeting
      time that turn into the years of our lives.

It should make us stop and think just how precious time
      is in our lives.
For we have wasted time, we have pleaded for time, we have lost
      time and needed time.
So why do we continue to allow time to run away and leave old
      wounds unattended?
Old wounds that keep stopping the stab of conscience that tells us
      to do right,
Where wrong is executed and life has gone astray.
Old wounds that make us stay stubborn, just because we want
      our way,
Old wounds that make us feel we are way beyond reproach,
Old wounds that blind us to another's need, justifying their
      circumstances to the life they lead.

Tick-tock, Tick-tock, the clock on the wall says it all.
For it reminds us that we are time travelers.
All of our lives spun into its web of minutes and hours, its days
      and nights.
These minutes and hours fill up the measure by which we live,
And, in it lies the sum total of our lives.
In it is our life story captured by the hands of time so we might
      understand.
We touch these moments only for a time.

For when we look with clear vision at how precious time is in
      our lives,
We will clean up our act, and will rearrange our plan,
Our view of life will take on a new perspective and a thirst for life
      begin,
Dragons that used to haunt us, we will make disappear, and we can
Resolve issues and scale mountains that we once refused to pass.
Best of all we will value the importance of time, as long as we can
Watch a pendulum swinging and hear the clock go tick-tock, tick-tock.

ANCHORED

Don't let life pass you by, anchored to daydreams
     of the past,
Holding on to your bag of what if, could have,
     should have and maybe.
Life is given to be lived, and we cannot anchor
     ourselves to a Well of regrets.

Time leaps forward with each New Year, and
     nothing can hold it back,
And whether we like it or not, there are some things
     we must let go.
Letting go is not forgetting, it's just putting things
     where they belong,
Into the file of memories, to the back of yesterday's
     shelf.

Only then will we breathe new life into us, to
     embrace tomorrow,
Only then can we start looking at life with a new
     measure of hope,
Only then will we welcome opportunities, that we
     could never see,
Only then will we understand in deserving life, we
     deserve to be the best that we can be.

MOVING ON

Why do we waste precious time in useless fears and worries,
      as to why our lives should be what it is not?
Why do we shed useless tears blaming others for our troubled lot,
And continue to wave our banner of unforgiveness around at
      every chance we have got?
Why do we berate ourselves, in spite of things we have, by constant
      hunger for things we haven't got?
Always demanding the most from life, but never asking ourselves
      what we are doing to be deserving of it?

This is the useless baggage to which we continually chain ourselves,
Its only purpose being to hinder us from moving forward, and to keep
      us always looking back.
There is no question that our life paths will take each one of us in
      a different direction,
Despite our good and bad, highs and lows, and the torment of
Inexplicable circumstances, for which reason will never find an answer.
The ups and downs, the roundabouts, the injustices for which logic
Will never find words to explain, nor which society can never ever repay.
The petty quarrels and feuds that lead to irreparable damage and harm.
The pain and indignities suffered, those joys short lived, the sorrows
Dispensed, the defeats encountered, and somewhere along the line
      our triumphs achieved.

Yet, there is a turning point, for somewhere amid the confusion of any
      life, you must come to a stop sign and turn a corner.
You must, or you will find yourself going around in circles doing the
Same things day after day and hauling around the same ball and chain.
How do I change this? you might ask, simply by – Start clearing out
      the corners of your life.
Close the door upon old nuisances and grudges, they have had their
Moment living themselves too many times over in your mind, the
      deed has been done, their time has expired.
Don't keep giving them a birthright every day, you are only cheating
      on your own life, subtracting little by little each day.

It is time to learn from your lessons of the past, so that your life will
Take a new turn, leading to more wiser and prosperous experiences.
We cannot erase the past, but we can move away from or close that
    window in time and redirect our paths.
We can learn to do new things and meet different kinds of people.

We can take an interest in new ideas, go to new places and keep
    educating our minds.
Moving on means, letting go of people, places or things that serve
    no good purpose in our lives,
Hard as it might seem to walk away from things that seem familiar,
It is harder yet to watch yourself belittled, your hopes gradually
    diminish and your dreams stifled.

Stop turning back the pages of yesterday, in a life that seem to
    be going nowhere,
Start looking for the sunrise and what you can make of it, instead
    of brooding at the sunset.
When bitterness or hate start to filter through your mind, think-
    Moving on.
When your life starts feeling like a revolving door with the same
    buzz of activity, think − Moving on.
When you see yourself continuing to make bad life choices,
    Think-Moving on,.
Or you will continue to fight the same phantoms every day until
You realize that moving on, is essential for growth and new things
    to happen.
Moving on is an elixir in many ways. It is seeing life with a new
enthusiasm, and whatever else it might be, it is surely self-discovery.

A MELODY

Strange, how haunting the sounds of a melody
             can be.
And how suddenly it can jog your memory.
Reminding you of a day, or night, or time of year,
Rekindling thoughts you can, or cannot bear to hear.

It can recall a mood, let you envision the place,
And if you were with someone, you can still see
             their face.
And as you listen to its haunting strain,
Round and round in your head, echoes the refrain.

Should it revive memories treasured and dear,
Even the faintest lilt of that melody you hear,
Will wrap itself again around your heart, and keep
             bringing to mind,
Things from which you never want to part.

Alas, if it should trigger memories of lost love or pain,
You may have no wish to listen to it again, still it
             will haunt you in some way,
For such memories upon which you had closed the
             door,
In that melody, will be brought to life once more.

IN FINDING TRANQUILITY

Enjoy the beauty of flowers,
The kind that can intoxicate you,
Whose fragrance pursues you here and there,
    engulfing everywhere.
Play sweet soft music when you seek to soothe
    a weary brain,
Let a shower of softly falling rain, gently misting
Your windowpane, lull you to sleep again and again.

Look to the ocean, and listen to its murmur in a
    seashell
Watch the might of the waves, as they surge up and
    swell,
Cast your thoughts out with the tide, believe that when
    it returns,
On it, new hope and energy will ride.

Indulge for a few minutes in daily meditation, for,
Life has for all of us demands that must be served.
And, so to harness outer strength, tune inward for
    guidance in all purpose or intent.
Close your eyes and lie at ease, shut out everything,
    until time just seem to cease.
Allow yourself to feel a sense of utter calm.
With the body now at rest, the spirit will be at God's
    command.

THE CIRCLE OF LIFE

Let us remember that life is a circle, going around,
      and coming around again.
As long as we live, no matter where or when,
The circle of life will take us through past, present,
      and future, again and again.

Each life will encounter in time- a battle to be fought,
      a victory to be gained,
A defeat to be overcome, a sacrifice that must be made,
A mountain that has to be climbed, a fear to conquer,
And a bridge to be crossed.

Each life will leave behind, a road to be forgotten,
Will look towards the beginning of a new horizon,
Will receive love and bestow love, will nurture hope
      yet entertain despair,
Will know the joy of acceptance, yet experience the
      pain of sorrow.

We will bask in the light of compliments,
Yet be swept through the wave of criticism,
We will enjoy moments of peace, yet endure moments
      of conflicts,
We will feel the sunshine of optimism, yet touch the
      darkness of pessimism,
We will feel like a failure at something, yet succeed
      at another,

The tide of life flows in both directions as it goes
      back and forth,
But we can keep our head above the water despite
      the current sweeping us about,
Two things we must cultivate to keep us solid as
      stone,
The courage to believe in ourselves, and perseverance
      to see us through.

TIME

Time like an elusive spinning wheel endlessly
          rushes on,
Trampling through our lives, on its flight to eternity.
If only we could stop one special moment in time,
          and hold on to it forever,
How different our lives might have been, by capturing
          that moment, we would have seen.

Then there would be no reason to look back with regrets,
At the moments, time have stolen away, moments we
          never wanted to let go,
But there was nothing we could do or say, moments that
          could have changed our lives,
Moments, we can never again capture with our eyes.

Time is our companion no matter what we do, sometimes
It proves a blessed friend, sometimes a foe we fear,
          when we feel it closing in.
Still, we cannot hold back the passage of time, it will follow
          wherever we go.
It dwells in our past, dominates our present, and even controls
          our future.
It inspires us, enlightens us, consumes us, and grips us to the end.

Time, the seasoned traveler stalks us day by day, helping or
          hindering as we go upon our way.
And so we are like prisoners meshed in by its power, even as we
          hope or despair, a minute or an hour.
We live the daily practice of our lives constantly over and over,
And like the elusive spinning wheel madly racing, Time we all
          are embracing.

VISION

Vision is the mirror of our mind,
From which we can fashion or invent,
Ideals we seek, or aspirations on which we
      are bent,
Like a flash of inspiration across our minds
        these images are sent.

Many a soul cast down in despair and broken,
Has mastered defeat, because of this good token,
Others have triumphed over doubt and fear,
Indebted only to vision, whose time had come,
        whose idea had to be born.

Vision like a seed when nurtured, brings forth its
        fruit in season,
Yet, if neglected withers for lack of being fed,
From the fires of human passion, it turns slowly,
To embers, then ashes that are cold and dead.

Still vision will always embrace ideas to come.
Seek to build on ideas that are, dare to climb where
        others have never been,
Will make a milestone in some life, or carve a place
        in history,
The likes of which was never before seen.

WHEN TIME STANDS STIILL

There is a moment in every life when time seems to stand
      still,
It is that moment when you are thrown off-guard by
Someone or something that leaves you speechless or
      dumbfounded.
It is that moment when life puts you squarely in the middle
Of the valley of decision, and you must search frantically
      for answers.

It might be a moment when time signals closing a door on a
      relationship,
That you have long endured, one which has undermined your
      morale.
Perhaps it is in a need for a detour to a different fork in the
      road, to a new chapter of your life,
Maybe it is in finding yourself confronted with a situation,
      crucial to your survival,
Or it could be standing up to an old adversary that has long
      intimidated you.
Someone who might have kept your mind a hostage limiting
      possibilities of all that you could do.

It might mean refusing to no longer be taken for granted,
Or being put down or spoken to in a disrespectful way.
It could be in that betrayal of trust or heartbreak that caught
      you by surprise,
Or a moment that you look back over your life, with regrets
      that made you want to cry,
Knowing you have to own up to your faults, or own self-
      worth to restore your dignity.

It is one life altering moment that makes you realize that
      things will, and must change,
And you have to decide how best to keep on living and

make your life feel worthwhile.

It will challenge you to take a leap of faith and reflect on
whatever you say or do, carefully.

Knowing that whatever you do, the winds of change will
blow,

For each of us in some direction, that compels us to take
charge of our lives,

More than ever, in that moment —When Time Stands Still.

AUTHOR'S NOTE

The author is always interested to know how her book has inspired her readers to motivate change in their lives, give hope, help themselves or help others, turn over a new leaf, or view life with a new perspective. Each day of our lives bring new experiences and we learn from each other as well as the experiences we encounter. The goal is to seek out how to overcome our challenges and know that we can surmount them. After the night, there is always daylight!